World Issues

Human Rights

Fiona Macdonald and Clare Weaver

Chrysalis Children's Books

WORLD ISSUES

ANIMAL RIGHTS
DRUGS
EQUAL OPPORTUNITIES
GENETIC ENGINEERING
GENOCIDE
HUMAN RIGHTS
POVERTY
RACISM
REFUGEES
TERRORISM

First published in the UK in 2003 by
Chrysalis Children's Books
The Chrysalis Building, Bramley Road, London W10 6SP

Editor: Clare Weaver
Editorial Manager: Joyce Bentley
Designer: Victoria Webb
Consultant: John Polley
Picture Researcher: Glass Onion Pictures

ISBN: 1 84138 878 5

British Library Cataloguing in Publication Data for this book is available from
the British Library.

A BELITHA BOOK

Printed in Hong Kong/China
10 9 8 7 6 5 4 3 2 1

Picture Acknowledgements
We wish to thank the following individuals and organizations for their help and
assistance, and for supplying material in their collections: Corbis *front cover* (Neal
Preston), 46 (Reza/Sygma); Exile Images 10 (J. Holmes), 19 (H. Davies), 30 (H. Davies);
Panos Pictures 36 (Dermot Tatlow); Popperfoto 1, 6 (Reuters), 7 (AFP/Joel Robine), 12, 15,
(PPP), 16, 21 (Reuters), 23 (Reuters), 24, 27 (Reuters), 29, 33, 34, 39 (Reuters), 40, 41, 45
(Reuters); Rex Features 3 (Ray Tang), 4–5 (Sipa), 5 top (Sipa), 5 bottom (Sipa), 22, 25 (Sipa),
28 (Sipa), 37, 43 (Ray Tang), 47 (ACT); Stourbridge News 35; Topham Picturepoint 5
middle (UPPA), 8 (UN), 9 (AP), 11 (Photonews Service), 13, 14 (Photri), 17, 18, 20 (AP), 26
(Josef Polleross/ImageWorks), 31 (Photonews Service), 32 (AP), 38 (John
Moore/ImageWorks), 42 (UPPA), 44 (Chapman). The pictures used in this book do not
necessarily show the actual people named in the case studies in the text.

CONTENTS

Rigoberta's Story

Rigoberta Menchu is from the Qiche indigenous people of Guatemala in Central America. In 1992, she won the Nobel Peace Prize for her work for human rights. She was the first indigenous person to receive this honour.

RIGOBERTA WAS BORN in 1959, in a small village where everyone was very poor. Her father and her brothers were labourers on coffee and cotton plantations. The work was hard – 15 hours a day – and two of her brothers died. One was poisoned by pesticide sprays and the other died from hunger. Rigoberta started work, aged 8, picking cotton. She had no chance to go to school.

The workers lived in crowded shacks, with no clean water or lavatories. Often, all they had to eat was roots and leaves. Rigoberta's mother worked as a midwife, helping women and their babies. Many of them died, too, from poor food or disease.

Indigenous people made up two-thirds of the Guatemalan population, but they had no civil rights. The government and wealthy farmers took over their land. Rigoberta's father joined with other labourers to protest. They formed the United Peasant Committee, to organize petitions and demonstrations, asking for human rights. They were arrested and imprisoned many times.

Rigoberta and her brother Petrocino joined in the protests. In 1979, Petrocino was kidnapped, tortured and burned alive. He was just 16 years old. The next year, her father and 38 other protest leaders died in a mysterious fire. Many people blamed the army for starting it. Rigoberta's mother was raped, then killed.

Rigoberta knew that her life was also in danger. In 1983, she escaped across the border to Mexico. She decided to tell the world what had happened to her family and to all the other protesters, by writing a book. Her message was simple: 'We are people and we want to be respected, not to be the victims of intolerance or racism.'

After her book was published, in 1984, Rigoberta decided to dedicate the rest of her life to campaigning for human rights. She used her Nobel Prize money to fund an organization, named after her father, to work for indigenous peoples' rights all round the world.

Three human rights heroes

Rigoberta is just one example of countless people across the world who have dedicated their lives to the cause of human rights.

EUROPE
Andrei Sakharov (1921–89) won the Nobel Peace Prize in 1975. He was a top nuclear physicist in the USSR (Soviet Union), who spoke out about human rights abuses under the Communist Soviet regime.

AFRICA
Leading churchman Desmond Tutu won the Nobel Peace Prize in 1984 for his tireless work campaigning against the policy of apartheid (segregation of white and black people) in South Africa.

ASIA
Aung San Suu Kyi won the Nobel Peace Prize in 1991 for her campaign against human rights abuses in Burma (Myanmar). An opponent of the military dictatorship in Burma, she was under house arrest from 1989 to 2002.

What Are Human Rights?

The idea of human rights sets basic standards of justice, dignity and respect for all humanity. It is closely linked to other important beliefs about how individuals should be treated and societies should be run, such as freedom, toleration and equal opportunities.

A campaigner tries to halt army tanks at a human rights protest in Beijing, China, June 1989. All round the world, men and women have risked their lives to stand up for human rights.

THERE ARE TWO different kinds of human rights. The first kind is things that people should be free to do, such as getting an education or taking part in politics. The second kind is things that people should be free from, such as discrimination or false imprisonment. Human rights belong to everyone, and cannot be taken away from any man, woman or child. All human rights are equally important and are linked to each other. We cannot pick and choose between them.

'Human rights are the rights a person has simply because he or she is a human being.'

'Human rights are held by all persons, equally, universally, and forever.'

Source: University of Michigan Human Rights Resource Center

Are human rights popular?

Human rights involve many sensitive issues, such as race and religion. They affect all levels of society, from strong government leaders to people without power, such as homeless refugees. They give individuals the right to challenge national laws and state institutions, such as the army or the police. Sometimes, they can seem dangerous, or too 'soft' – even murderers have human rights. For all these reasons, human rights can be controversial or deeply unpopular. Human rights organizations are often criticized by politicians and the media, and human rights campaigners are sometimes attacked.

Human rights ideas help protect vulnerable people, like these Iraqi women and children driven from their homes by bombing raids in 1991.

This book will look at how and why the idea of human rights became increasingly powerful during the twentieth century, and at the part it plays in our world today. It will explore the way in which human rights – or the lack of them – have a big impact on all our everyday lives. It will also investigate how different individuals and organizations work to make sure that everyone, everywhere, can enjoy equal human rights.

Human rights workers face danger

Ita Nadia is a human rights activist working in Indonesia. She is a member of the National Commission on Violence Against Women and is co-ordinator of a team investigating the large-scale military-backed massacre of Indonesian Communist Party (PKI) members and its sympathisers in 1965, following an attempted coup, which was blamed on the PKI. It can be a dangerous job, but she is determined to continue with the investigation.

'After the National Commission of Human Rights set up those teams ... I received two calls, that terrorised me, that [said] that it is very, very dangerous for you to be involved in this team. And this man who called me ... he really tried to make me frightened. I'm working for the human rights. To open the history of the violations [abuses] of human rights and break the silence ... it will give detail on how the people have been violated, have been humiliated...'

Source: 'Asia Pacific', Australian Broadcasting Company

Who decides what human rights are?

To answer this question, governments, lawyers and campaigners refer to the words of a historic document – the Universal Declaration of Human Rights (UDHR). It was the first internationally-agreed statement of human rights and is still very important today.

The Universal Declaration was drawn up by a Commission (working group) appointed by the United Nations (an organization of countries set up after the end of World War II to promote international peace and co-operation). It was agreed in 1948, after almost three years of discussions between the 58 nations that were members of the United Nations at that time.

The Declaration set out 30 rights that people everywhere should be able to enjoy. These include life, liberty and security – the basis for all other rights – plus freedom from slavery. It banned torture and cruel, inhuman or degrading (shameful) punishments for prisoners. It stated that everyone should have the right to a fair trial by impartial judges, and that they should not be unfairly arrested, detained or exiled. Criminals should be presumed innocent until proved guilty. It also outlawed discrimination 'of any kind, such as race, colour, sex, language, religion, political or other opinion, national or social origin, property, birth or other status.'

The Commission that drew up the Universal Declaration of Human Rights was headed by Eleanor Roosevelt (1884–1962), widow of the 32nd president of the USA and a long-time campaigner for disadvantaged people. She is shown here holding a copy of the Declaration, in 1949.

'All human beings are born free and equal in dignity and rights. They are endowed [born with] reason and conscience and should act towards one another in a spirit of brotherhood.'

Source: Universal Declaration of Human Rights, 1948

In 1949, members of the General Assembly of the United Nations met in New York to lay the foundation stone for a new headquarters building – a world centre for human rights.

The Universal Declaration also said that governments should not interfere unfairly in people's lives, and that all men and women should have the right to be full citizens in the land where they were born. They should be able to travel, and to leave their country, and to seek asylum (refuge) if they fear persecution. They should be free to marry and have a family, and own property. They should also be able to express their own religious beliefs and political ideas. They should be allowed to join together with others holding similar views, and to take part in government. State-run services, such as schools and hospitals, should be open to all citizens, whatever their political or religious opinions.

Finally, the Universal Declaration set out each individual's rights to seek work, to have equal pay, and to be given time off for rest and leisure. It said that everyone should have the right to an adequate standard of living – that is, food, water and shelter – and to receive benefits from state welfare systems (where they exist). It also stated that each person should have the right to education, and to take part in the cultural life of their community.

DEBATE – Do citizens have responsibilities in return for human rights?

- Yes. We should not have human rights if we are not good citizens.
- No. Everyone should be entitled to human rights, however well or badly they behave.

How Can Human Rights Be Achieved?

The Universal Declaration of Human Rights describes human rights very clearly. But it is only words and, by themselves, words have no power. They need to be put into practice. How can this be done?

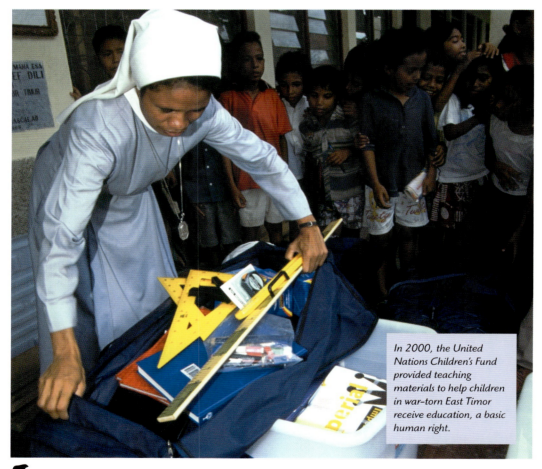

In 2000, the United Nations Children's Fund provided teaching materials to help children in war-torn East Timor receive education, a basic human right.

GOVERNMENTS CAN INCLUDE human rights ideas in their national laws. This may mean amending (changing) old laws, or passing new ones. Sometimes, countries join together to do this. For example, in 1981, many African states jointly agreed an African Charter on Human and People's Rights.

Are there international agreements?

Governments can also sign legally binding documents, in which they promise to uphold human rights. These documents are called treaties or covenants. If a country signs a covenant, but does not follow it, other nations can take action, and even go to war, against the offending country.

Since 1948, when the UDHR was first agreed, its ideas have been included in two powerful international treaties: the International Covenant on Civil and Political Rights (1966), and the International Covenant on Economic, Social and Cultural Rights (1976). There are also over 20 other treaties, covering the human rights of particular groups.

People power

Although they have no official status, individual human rights activists, like those featured on pages 4 and 5, and non-governmental organizations, such as Amnesty International and Human Rights Watch, have probably done more than anyone else to improve human rights all round the world. They work by exposing human rights abuses, creating damaging publicity for abusers and campaigning for change. Compared with them, United Nations human rights organizations can often seem hesitant and slow.

Can the United Nations take action?

The United Nations (UN) can check how much each nation is doing to advance human rights. It can ask governments to submit regular reports, describing their past action on human rights and their plans for the future. The UN also listens to complaints of human rights abuses and it can send Special Representatives to human rights trouble-spots around the world. In 1994, the United Nations created a new, very senior position – High Commissioner – to monitor human rights worldwide.

The Security Council (a group of 15 UN member states established to sort out threats to world peace) can also set up International Tribunals (special law-courts) to prosecute crimes against human rights. It can even send troops to stop human rights abuses.

The United Nations has also set up inter-governmental organizations – including UNICEF (United Nations Children's Fund) and WHO (World Health Organization) – which work to improve human rights. They collect money, provide information, raise awareness and send teams of experts to work in dangerous and difficult regions.

Supporters of human rights organization Amnesty International protest in London, 1998.

Do we all accept the same rights?

The Universal Declaration of Human Rights aims to be 'a common standard of achievement for all peoples and all nations'. Most countries have signed up to at least one of the many international treaties on human rights, but not everyone agrees to all of them. The USA and Somalia, for example, have not ratified (put into practice) the Convention on the Rights of the Child.

Why doesn't everyone agree?

There are several different reasons. Many governments see the UN's international covenants as a threat to their own independence. They do not want other governments, or UN organizations, interfering with their customs or their laws.

Some Asian and African nations see human rights covenants as the products of modern Western civilization. They believe the treaties are based on Western social, religious and political ideas, which are alien to their cultures. Malaysia's Prime Minister argued that the Universal Declaration of Human Rights' emphasis on individual rights, rather than responsibility to the community, made it unsuited to Asia, where community relationships are seen as most important. To solve this 'culture clash', some nations have suggested alternative ways of advancing human rights, such as the Cairo Declaration on Human Rights in Islam, agreed by a group of Muslim states in 1990. This sets out rules to protect human rights that are acceptable to most Muslims.

Prisoners at Camp X–Ray, Guantanamo Bay, Cuba, in 2002. Human rights protesters have criticized the US government for locking up suspects here without trial.

Delegates from many different nations lighting a Peace Torch at the United Nations Women's Conference in Beijing, China, 1995. The UN organizes regular international meetings like this, to discuss how to improve human rights worldwide.

Do governments fear human rights?

Many governments, all round the world, fear that including the Universal Declaration of Human Rights in their laws will be a threat to state security. It might give protesters, terrorists and other criminals too much freedom. This is especially the case since the 11 September 2001 terrorist attacks on the USA. Following that incident, the US government, led by President George W. Bush, imprisoned many Muslim men suspected of being involved in terrorist activities, at the US naval base at Guantanamo Bay in Cuba. The aim was to detain suspected terrorists before they had a chance to commit any crimes.

In other cases, undemocratic government leaders oppose human rights because they are frightened of losing power. They do not want to let ordinary people play a full part in government in case they elect someone else.

Are some human rights valued more?

Until the late 1980s, Communist countries, such as the USSR, argued that economic, social and cultural rights were more important than political ones. Communist governments made sure their citizens had good healthcare and education, but punished them for taking part in political protests, and denied them the right to travel abroad. In contrast, the USA said that political rights, especially free speech and freedom of conscience, were more important than economic or social ones. American governments did not think it was their duty to feed and house their citizens, or to provide them with more than a basic healthcare system.

Have People Always Had Human Rights?

Early law-codes tell us that people living long ago already had strong opinions about what a 'good' society should be like. In return for obeying the law, they expected certain rights.

Signing the United States' Declaration of Independence, 4 July 1776.

THE FIRST-KNOWN government law-code dates from around 1790 BC. It was made by Hammurabi, king of Babylon, in the Middle East. Others, like the Jewish Ten Commandments (written down around 1000 BC), the Hindu Vedas (from around 800 BC) or the Sayings of the Chinese philosopher Kung Futze (from around 500 BC), tell us that lawmakers from these times expected people to treat their fellow humans with dignity and to help needy members of their community. Many early societies had traditions such as the Jewish and Christian 'golden rule', which stated: 'Do unto others as you would have them do unto you'. Similar teachings are found in the Christian New Testament 'Love your neighbour as yourself' and the Muslim holy book, the Qur'an.

What other evidence is there?

Documents like the Magna Carta (1215), drawn up as a result of a quarrel between King John of England and powerful people in his country, laid down principles such as 'rulers are not above the law'. In 1776, the United States' Declaration of Independence stated that 'all men are created equal'. During the French Revolution, which began in 1789, anti-monarchy protesters drew up a 'Declaration of the Rights of Man and the Citizen'. In 1848, over 200 women met at Seneca Falls, USA, to draw up a 'bill of rights' detailing the social, civil and religious rights of women. In 1863, US President Abraham Lincoln issued the 'Emancipation Proclamation', which declared slaves to be 'forever free'.

When did nations come together?

In 1919, after the end of World War I, Britain, France and the USA organized an international peace conference in Paris. Delegates proposed that the defeated ruler of Germany, Kaiser Wilhelm II, be put on trial for a 'supreme offence against international morality' for his role in bringing about war. This was the first time ever that a country's war-leader had been accused of crimes against human rights.

The peace treaties signed at the end of the conference called for international protection for the rights of life, liberty and freedom of religion. More importantly, they created the League of Nations – an organization that would work for international peace and co-operation. Amongst other things, it called for the fair treatment of ordinary people and it set up worldwide medical campaigns to end disease.

In the first half of the twentieth century, human rights campaigner Mahatma Gandhi (1869–1948) led many non–violent protests to call for independence for India and international peace.

After World War II ended in 1945, an international tribunal was set up to try Nazi leaders (seated, in centre) accused of war crimes. This was one of the first-ever attempts by the international community to use the law to enforce human rights.

Why were today's covenants created?

During the twentieth century, a succession of wars and revolutions made many people keen to develop international organizations that would work to reduce conflict, and limit the harm done, especially to civilians.

The League of Nations was a brave experiment, but it failed. Member nations refused to let international projects interfere with their own plans. This meant that the League was powerless against Nazi Germany, one of the most savage twentieth-century violators of human rights. From 1933, the Nazi government began to exterminate men and women with mental or physical disabilities, and to persecute many minority groups, including Jews and gypsies.

World War II began in 1939, with Britain, France, Russia, and later the USA, fighting against Nazi Germany and its allies. The war ended in 1945 but, long before that, government leaders had declared their commitment to human rights. For example, in 1941, US President Roosevelt declared that 'Four Freedoms' were essential for all people: freedom of speech and religion, freedom from want and freedom from fear.

Women in Chile, South America, campaigning for democracy in 1989. The same year, public pressure forced dictator Augusto Pinochet to give up power.

What other movements played a role?

In 1945, the League of Nations was replaced by the United Nations Organization, which drew up the Universal Declaration of Human Rights in 1948. Since then, human rights ideas have been encouraged in many different ways.

In the 1950s and 1960s, leaders of Asian and African countries began to demand independence from their European colonial rulers, and many based their campaigns on human rights ideas. At the same time, civil rights leaders in the USA, such as Martin Luther King Jr., called for an end to racial discrimination. In the 1970s, liberation movements in South America demanded freedom from dictatorship,

'Injustice anywhere is a threat to justice everywhere.'

American civil rights leader Martin Luther King Jr. (1929–68)

and called for international brotherhood. From the 1960s to the 1990s, feminist movements campaigned for women's rights. Gay pride campaigners have also linked their aims for personal freedom to wider issues of human rights.

These campaigning groups did not always achieve their aims, but they created a network of human rights movements, and kept alive the hope of universal human rights.

How Do Human Rights Ideas Affect People?

Ideas about human rights can be powerful. They can give hope to people who are being wrongly treated. They can inspire people to work to make the world a better place, where there will be freedom, peace and justice for everyone.

WHATEVER COUNTRY WE live in, our lives are affected by ideas about human rights. If we live in a country that supports them, we have a much better chance of living the sort of life we want, in safety. If we live in a country that opposes human rights ideas, our lives will be restricted and, possibly, full of fear.

Black protesters occupying a 'whites only' railway carriage in South Africa, 1952. The South African policy of apartheid (racial segregation) denied all non-white people their human rights.

How are individuals affected?

Human rights ideas can influence all aspects of our lives, even the most private. For example, in 2002, a British transsexual born as a man but now living as a woman, won a case at the European Court of Human Rights after the British government refused to issue a new passport with her new gender identity. British law insisted that the passport should record the fact that she had been born a man. The European Court of Human Rights ruled that this violated her right to human dignity.

How are large groups helped?

Human rights ideas can also change what happens during large-scale public events, such as war. In June 2002, for example, the United Nations sent a Special Representative to visit the Russian republic of Chechnya, whose people are fighting for independence from Russia. He toured refugee camps and rough shelters to observe the conditions of children who had been driven out of their homes in the fighting. The Special Representative's visit put pressure on the Russian government, and on the local governors in Chechnya, to do all they could to make sure that children were given their human rights to food, shelter, education and safety.

A success story from Iran

Iran's decision to suspend the punishment of death by stoning for adultery, made in response to the 'demands of the modern age' and mounting protests inside and outside the country ... signals a victory for reformist MPs who have been looking to end discrimination against women. The move comes after pressure from the European Union, which is engaged in human rights talks linked to trade negotiations...

Under Iran's strict Islamic law, in place since the 1979 Islamic Revolution, men and women convicted of adultery are normally sentenced to death by stoning... According to the law, the stones must be big enough to injure but not kill with just a few blows, which Amnesty International has described as a 'method specifically designed to increase the victim's suffering.'

Source: IPS–Inter Press Service, 2001

A Gay Pride march in Brighton, UK. Gay Pride campaigners have used human rights ideas to fight for equality and acceptance.

Do human rights ideas help nations?

Some of the earliest and most successful human rights campaigns were concerned with peoples' rights to 'self-determination' – that is, to decide what the future of their nations should be.

Ideas about human rights helped many peoples to win independence from rule by stronger foreign countries – although their human rights aims were often mixed with the ambition for political power. For example, guerrillas in Malaya fought a long war against British colonial rulers from 1945–57. They wanted their human right to political freedom, but also to impose strict Communist rule.

Many leaders of newly independent colonies also began their political careers as campaigners for human rights. For example, Nigerian activist Nnamdi Azikiwe organized local groups, calling for political, workers' or educational rights, into a powerful National Council, which helped negotiate a new Nigerian Constitution with the British government. He became the first president of the independent republic of Nigeria in 1963.

Later, human rights ideas inspired some Communist-run nations in Eastern Europe to try and break free from Soviet (Russian) control, and govern themselves. In 1977, a Czech protest group called 'Charter 77' began a long campaign for human rights. In 1989, Czech Communist rulers were finally removed from power, and Vaclav Havel, the leader of Charter 77, became president of Czechoslovakia.

Human rights protesters attack a statue of Soviet dictator Josef Stalin in the Czech capital, Prague, in 1989. The placard around Stalin's neck reads 'Nothing lasts forever'.

International experts examine a mass grave in Serbia, 1996. It contains the bodies of some of the 8000 Muslims who were killed after Serb forces attacked the supposedly 'safe' city of Srebrenica.

What happens in national struggles?

Peoples' rights to nationality, and to residence within their home states, can be threatened. For example, in Bosnia in the 1990s, Serbian nationalist movements began 'ethnic cleansing', to remove Muslims from the province of Kosovo, where they had lived for hundreds of years. To help the persecuted families regain their human rights to a nationality and a homeland, the United Nations imposed sanctions on the Serbian warlords who controlled Bosnia, and provided food and medical supplies to help refuges. But this was not enough to protect the Muslims' human rights. In 1995, the United Nations sent a Task Force of soldiers to restore law and order, while leading members of the UN Security Council, led by the USA, forced the Serbians to end their abuse of human rights.

DEBATE - Should international organizations, like the United Nations, take action against countries to halt the abuse of human rights?

- Yes. The international community has a duty to protect human rights. Unless it acts, many innocent people will be harmed.
- No. Foreigners should not interfere in any other country.

Do human rights help workers?

United Nations' covenants guarantee workers many different rights, including freedom from discrimination, fair working conditions and the right to join workers' associations. They totally outlaw slavery or forced labour of any kind – of prisoners, for example, who may be made to work in prison in order to 'qualify' for food. Some human rights campaigners also argue that workers should be free to refuse to work on projects – such as weapons manufacture – that might be used to deny other peoples' human rights.

United Nations' covenants also require workers doing equal jobs to be given equal pay, and many nations have included these rules in their national law. Some countries, such as the UK, Australia and the USA, have also made laws setting a minimum wage level. Workers who believe they are being paid unfairly can appeal to law courts or special tribunals to protect their rights.

How does globalization affect workers?

Multinational corporations often look for the cheapest places to manufacture goods that will be sold worldwide. These businesses are not bound by any one nation's laws. Instead, they seek to create the maximum profit for their shareholders. Sometimes, they deliberately site factories in countries where human rights laws are weak. They claim this gives them greater flexibility. To help workers, some governments have tried to persuade corporations to obey laws protecting workers' rights by setting up groups

In 1977, women workers employed by the Grunwick company in London, UK, went on strike to support their demand to belong to a trade union. They wanted the union to represent them in negotiations with company management, and to help safeguard their other interests, such as health and safety. The right to belong to a trade union is set out in the United Nations Charter of Human Rights, but workers in many countries have found it very difficult to achieve.

Teenage boys and girls working in a garment factory, Bangladesh. Some countries, like Bangladesh, rely so heavily on factories like these to earn export income, that they are unwilling to enforce workers' human rights.

such as the Apparel Industry Partnership in the USA– a group of clothing manufacturers who agree to treat workers well. In return, they are more likely to win government contracts – and get good publicity.

Can anyone else help workers?

The most successful campaigners for workers' rights have been non-governmental organizations that monitor worldwide labour conditions and report on them. Consumer groups have also been very effective – such as the American students who refused to buy their school and college wear from companies that treated their workers unfairly.

Sweatshop conditions

Publishing this report on a famous brand sports footwear factory in Vietnam forced the company to improve workers' rights.
'Thousands of young women, mostly under 25, work over 10 hours a day, six days a week, in terrible heat and noise, with only polluted air to breathe... Wages are very low – around US$10 [about £7] a week. Many of the workers who handle dangerous chemicals do not wear masks or gloves...'
Source: Human Rights Watch World Report, 2000

Non–governmental organizations, like the Grameen Bank in South Asia, help women escape from poverty by lending them small amounts of money. This woman has used her loan to buy a mobile phone, which she charges other villagers a fee to use.

What about women and children?

Women make up the majority of the world's population, but nowhere are they completely equal with men. In Kuwait and Saudi Arabia, they have no legal independence. In Thailand, Ukraine and Moldova, they are forced to work in the sex industry. Millions of women have been raped by soldiers in Kosovo, Rwanda and Sierra Leone. Even in places like Europe and the USA, women are still often paid less than men for doing exactly the same job.

Most nations claim to value their young people, yet UN data shows that one or two babies out of every ten die before they are five years old. That is a total of over 23 million each year. If they survive, young children may be forced to work, beg or serve as soldiers. Many face bullying, neglect or sexual abuse.

Can anyone help?

In spite of these grim statistics, human rights ideas are helping to improve women's and children's lives. Powerful UN Committees can put pressure on governments by asking for reports on progress towards rights. For example, in 2001, a representative from Morocco reported on new basic literacy programmes for women, along with help to find jobs and micro-credit schemes, which lend small amounts of money to very poor people. These schemes allow people to help themselves, by giving them the means to set up community enterprises. A Brazilian representative urged other nations to follow his country's example of giving money to poor families to make it possible for their children to go to school instead of to work. That way, the children get their human right to education, and with it the chance of a better future, but their families can still afford to buy food – another basic human right.

Many children are denied their human rights because of poverty

'I sell spices and palm oil in a small market in the mornings. In the afternoon, I'm at school. I work because my father's salary isn't enough to support us.'

Ruth Meta, aged 16, Democratic Republic of Congo
Source: Save the Children annual review 2000/2001

Why is progress so slow?

Despite these examples of progress, it has been difficult to persuade many traditional societies to give up customs that abuse women's and children's rights. In the 1990s, one Masai woman from Kenya took her husband to court for beating her so severely that she needed hospital treatment. She was supported by the Kenyan Branch of the International Federation of Women Lawyers. They wanted the public to recognize that wife-beating was against human rights. The woman won her case, but now she says: 'Women are very angry with me … it is unheard of in Masailand to put your husband into jail.'

A child soldier tells his story

'The army was a nightmare. We suffered greatly from the cruel treatment we received. We were constantly beaten, mostly for no reason at all, just to keep us in a state of terror. I still have a scar on my lip and sharp pains in my stomach from being brutally kicked by the older soldiers... They forced me to learn how to fight the enemy, in a war that I didn't understand why was being fought.'

Emilio, recruited by the Guatemalan army, age 14
Source: Testimony given at a Congressional briefing on child soldiers, sponsored by Human Rights Watch, Washington DC, USA, 1997

This young boy in India has a dangerous job – operating fast-moving spinning machines. In developing countries, many families rely on children to help earn enough money to survive.

What about people with disabilities?

Over 600 million people all round the world live with disability. Their experiences vary, but they all face some kind of discrimination, such as lack of employment opportunities. This is often caused by ignorance or prejudice. In many countries, people with disabilities are doubly disadvantaged. They share their fellow-citizens' problems of poverty or repressive government, and have extra difficulties, caused by disability, as well. Old people, who are no longer fit and strong, often face similar discrimination.

What has the UN done?

The United Nations has been working to achieve human rights for people with disabilities since the 1980s, setting out various international rules intended to help bring about disability rights. In 2002, it announced plans for a Convention (treaty with force of law) on the rights of Persons with Disabilities, and appointed a high-ranking official (a Special Rapporteur) to monitor disability rights worldwide.

Who else is working for disability rights?

In some countries, disabled people are still treated as if they are less than human, and denied almost all rights. In 2002, for example, human rights campaigning group Amnesty International called for international protests against conditions in Bulgaria. There, people with mental or physical disabilities are shut away in homes and hospitals, described as 'worse than prison'. Some are forced to submit to treatment against their will; others die 'as a result of gross neglect'.

How do human rights ideas help?

Human rights ideas have had a powerful impact. They have inspired many campaigners to argue that people with disabilities, and old people as well, are not people 'in need', who should be helped for kindly or charitable reasons. Instead, they are people with just the same human rights as other members of society, whose rights – for example, to work, to suitable housing, or to travel – are often rationed or denied.

Bored, confused and frightened, four disabled children share one cot in a Romanian orphanage, in 2000. Parents in many countries abandon babies with disabilities, because they feel unable to cope with them.

In 1997, these disabled rights campaigners staged a dramatic protest against planned welfare reforms outside 10 Downing Street, the home of the British prime minister.

BLAIR SCROOGES DISABLED PEOPLE

BLAIR DOES'NT CARE

Old people deserve rights

'Older persons are the custodians [keepers] of our traditions, our heritage and our cultures. They reflect our past and are mirrors of our future. They have the right to a healthy, productive life, to live in a caring environment, and to be treated with respect.'

Source: Zola Skweyiya, Minister of Social Development in South Africa

Do Human Rights Ideas Improve Justice?

Without a fair system of justice to regulate society, there can be no human rights. Laws set standards for human rights in each country. Judges, the police and prison staff make sure that laws are obeyed. If there are unjust laws, or corrupt judges and officials, then human rights are likely to be ignored.

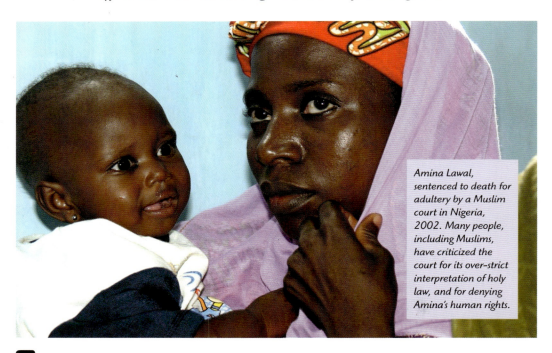

Amina Lawal, sentenced to death for adultery by a Muslim court in Nigeria, 2002. Many people, including Muslims, have criticized the court for its over-strict interpretation of holy law, and for denying Amina's human rights.

THE UNIVERSAL DECLARATION of Human Rights states that 'All are equal before the law', and that everyone is entitled to a fair trial. It adds that no one should be arrested without reasonable suspicion, and everyone should be presumed innocent until they are proved to have committed a crime.

'It is every government's duty to ensure law and order for the benefit of all citizens, but this cannot be imposed at the expense of the basic rights of the people.'

Source: Amnesty International, 2002

Is justice always fair?

In countries with violent or repressive rulers, judges, police and court officials are themselves accused of human rights crimes. Often the armed forces are involved as well. Sometimes, human rights violations happen when a government feels that it is facing an emergency, such as a sudden rise in crime. Sometimes, they are used as a brutal way of silencing the opposition, and staying in power.

Human rights organizations keep a careful lookout for human rights crimes. For example, in October 2002, Amnesty International called for the government of Bangladesh 'to investigate immediately all allegations of deaths in custody and torture by the army and police since a 'crackdown' on crime – known as Operation Clean Heart – began.' Amnesty claimed that many alleged wrongdoers had needed hospital treatment after beatings, and that some

had died. Some of the people arrested were known offenders, but others belonged to opposition political parties, and had never been linked to any crime.

Careful monitoring and international appeals cannot force any government to change its behaviour, but they can bring unwelcome publicity, and encourage respect for human rights.

What about prisoners?

Today, there are probably more prisoners, in more crowded prisons, than ever before. Often, prison conditions are grim, with small, dirty cells and primitive sanitation. Attacks by warders or other prisoners are common. Human Rights Watch, a campaigning organization that monitors conditions in prisons, commented, 'We believe that a government's claim to respect human rights should be assessed … by how it treats its prisoners, including those not held for political reasons.'

In 1997, Romanian prisoners protested against cramped conditions, like these, where 51 men had to share one small room.

DEBATE - Is it ever right to put people in prison before they have had a fair trial?

* Yes. Sometimes, governments need to lock up people suspected of terrorism or other dangerous crimes.
* No. It is a serious abuse of human rights to imprison people who have not been convicted of any crime.

Children having fun at a multi-cultural carnival in Brighton, UK, in 2001. Multi-cultural education can help stop discrimination and promote human rights, as children studying and playing together learn to respect each other's ideas, traditions and beliefs.

Racist attacks

- In 1999, 41 people died as victims of racist violence in Europe.
- Throughout the 1990s, there were an estimated 130 000 violent racist incidents each year in the UK alone.

Source: oneworld.net 2002

Can discrimination be stopped?

Many countries have passed laws incorporating the Universal Declaration's ban on 'discrimination of any kind'. Yet despite this, discrimination on grounds of race, caste, tribe, religion and many other causes, is still widespread.

Who checks anti-discrimination laws?

The United Nations has the power to examine each member nation's laws, to make sure that they do not violate human rights. For example, in August 2000, the UN announced that it was 'concerned … that the national legislation [laws] of Yemen did not contain explicit provisions [clear rules] prohibiting discrimination on the grounds of race or ethnic origin'. In Senegal, it recommended the government take action 'to promote understanding, tolerance and friendship among racial and ethnic groups'.

However, it can often be difficult to make nations accept criticism and improve human rights. In 1997, after the UN criticized Australia's treatment of Aboriginal children, the Australian Prime Minister angrily replied, 'Australia decides what happens in this country through the laws and parliaments of Australia. I mean in the end we are not told what to do by anybody. We make our own moral judgements...'

Who puts laws into action?

Many nations now have independent 'watchdogs' to monitor the impact of their anti-discrimination laws, such as the Human Rights Bureau in the US Department of State, or the Commission for Racial Equality in the UK. Campaigning groups have set up international networks, such as UNITED, in Europe, which has 450 member organizations in 43 countries, and links with over 1000 similar organizations worldwide. There are even special campaigning groups dedicated to checking sites on the Internet, since communication via the World Wide Web makes it much easier for racists to spread their anti-human rights message and escape anti-discrimination laws.

DEBATE - Are human rights policies really necessary?

- Yes. They protect people from unjust laws and unfair attitudes.
- No. We should trust governments to make their own decisions.

In countries that support the United Nations Declaration on Human Rights, citizens who feel they have been discriminated against can ask the courts to punish people who have harmed them, or denied them their human rights. For example, in 1998, Royal Marine Mark Parchment sued the British Army in the High Court. He alleged that other Marines had beaten and tortured him, because of his ethnic origins.

Do human rights ideas bring freedom?

There are many kinds of freedom – from the personal to the political – protected by the Universal Declaration for Human Rights. These include freedom to choose a marriage partner, freedom of thought, conscience and religion, freedom to speak a local language and freedom to elect a government. Because 'freedom' can mean so many things, it is often difficult to enforce by law.

Do human rights help in other ways?

They can set standards to aim for, and they inspire courage and hope. For example, women forced by family pressure to marry against their will can appeal to women's groups who work to support human rights. Even though these groups cannot change traditional attitudes, they can provide information, counselling and legal advice – and perhaps a safe place to hide.

Just occasionally, human rights ideas can help bring a complete change of policy. This has happened in many remote European regions, where people have increasingly claimed the right to speak local languages as part of a wider campaign to be free from central government control. In Scotland, for example, in the early twentieth century, the native Gaelic language was banned in government schools, and children who spoke it were beaten. Today, Gaelic is taught in many Scottish schools, and there are government-sponsored newspapers, television and radio stations created specially for Gaelic-speakers.

Is free speech always welcome?

Sometimes, the human right to freedom of speech can seem very uncomfortable. For example, a well-known French historian denied that the Holocaust (the deliberate massacre of millions of Jews by German Nazis during World War II) had taken place. The government of France threatened to prosecute him for racial and religious discrimination. In return, he accused the French government of abusing his human right to free speech. But the European Human Rights Commission ruled that the government had been correct. It said that the right to freedom of speech did exist, but it could not be used to violate other human rights, such as freedom from discrimination.

In 1945, Russian writer Alexandr Solzhenitsyn was sent to work in brutal labour camps for daring to criticize the Soviet government. But he refused to be silenced. After he was released in 1956, he published powerful novels that told the world how the Soviet government denied citizens their human rights.

In 1994, some Muslim high-school students in Lille, France, caused controversy by wearing headscarves to lessons. This was against French laws, which ban all religious symbols from schools. Public opinion was divided – were the laws fair to members of all faiths, or did they deny Muslim students their rights?

Discrimination against Muslim women

In 1999, Merve Kavacki was elected to the Turkish parliament, but she was refused permission to take the oath and play a full part in debates because she insisted on wearing the *hijab* (Muslim woman's clothing, which covers the head and body; *hijab* means modest dress). At least 75 per cent of Turkish women wear the *hijab*, but they are banned from wearing it in public offices and institutes of higher education. Merve said: 'In the twenty-first century they [Turkish government] must allow us this freedom... My head is covered because of my faith. I will defend my rights until the end.'

Source: Crescent International, May 1999

Ruud Lubbers, United Nations Commissioner for Human Rights, greets Afghan refugee children at a camp in Pakistan in 2001.

Child refugees speak out

'I would like to say to those who oppose refugees not to prejudge before they get to know us... We did not have a choice about where to go: there was no water, no food and you could not choose where to go – you could only search for a way out.'

Somalian girl, aged 14

'We only left because it was a matter of life and death for my parents ... we were respectable people ... otherwise my parents say we would never have left our own country to come to a strange country and have stones thrown at us by children in the street. However, my sisters and I really appreciate this country, because we have got our freedom and our rights. Freedom is a human right.'

Kosovan girl, aged 16

Source: I Didn't Come Here for Fun, *report by Save the Children and Scottish Refugee Council*

Do human rights ideas aid refugees?

The Universal Declaration states that 'everyone has a right to seek and to enjoy in other countries asylum from persecution'. But this human right is often challenged by nations where refugees seek to settle, even when their governments have agreed to protect the rights of refugees and asylum seekers. For example, in the late 1990s, the UK, France and other European nations detained hundreds of asylum seekers, or tried to expel them. Many of these people were desperate after years of suffering in their homelands, and they risked their lives trying to find a safe place to live. In just four years in the late 1990s, over 600 people were drowned, suffocated or frozen to death as they tried to enter Europe illegally. Campaigning groups, and individual lawyers, help some refugees challenge

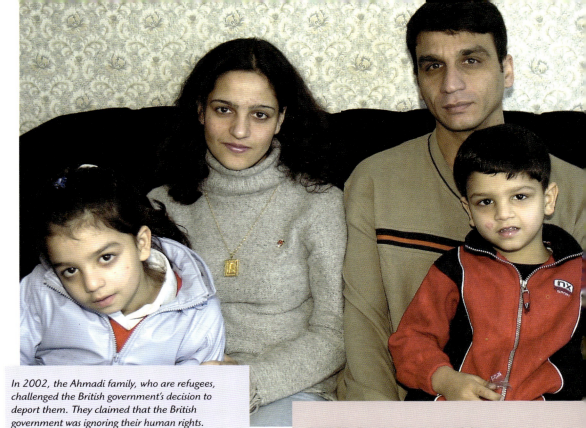

In 2002, the Ahmadi family, who are refugees, challenged the British government's decision to deport them. They claimed that the British government was ignoring their human rights.

government actions in court. But this was – and is – a slow and expensive process, and national laws are often carefully drafted to stay just within the provisions of the United Nations rules.

Why do governments refuse refugees?

Governments and politicians in wealthy countries are often unwilling to accept refugees because they believe most are not 'in genuine need of asylum'. They argue that they are 'economic migrants' (people searching for work) instead, and that they will be a 'burden' to the host community. Campaigners working with asylum seekers point out that migrants have often benefited their new home nations. For example, in Germany from 1988–92, immigrants generated 6 per cent of the country's gross national income.

DEBATE - Do we have a moral duty to accept asylum seekers driven from their homes by war?

- Yes. These people have been caught up in terrible circumstances through no fault of their own. Their families may have been killed and they have lost their homes and possessions. They deserve our help.
- No. Countries do not have a duty to help people from other nations. It is difficult enough to provide food, shelter and jobs for our own citizens, without having to provide aid for asylum seekers, as well.

Why Don't We All Have Human Rights?

In spite of hard work by the United Nations, and by many individuals, governments and campaigning organizations, millions of people still do not have basic human rights. Why is this?

Chinese troops outside the Potala Palace in Lhasa, Tibet, in 2000. The palace was home to the Dalai Lama, the Tibetan spiritual and political leader, until 1959, when he was forced to escape to India after a failed Tibetan uprising against Chinese rule. Since then, Chinese troops have destroyed many of Tibet's finest old buildings.

SOMETIMES, POWERFUL PEOPLE do not want to give others equality, justice or freedom, usually for political reasons. For example, in 2002, Human Rights Watch campaigners brought the case of Farid Tukhbatullin, an environmental activist from Turkmenistan, to the world's attention. Tukhbatullin was arrested and detained by the Turkmenistan authorities – Human Rights Watch say he is being persecuted for attending a conference on human rights in Moscow, and 'the diplomatic community should work together to ensure he is not harmed and is released immediately'. Turkmenistan, a former Soviet republic in central Asia, tolerates no opposition and crushes any criticism. It has banned any free media (newspapers, television or radio), opera, ballet and the circus.

Do we always know about abuses?

Sometimes, lack of information stops the growth of human rights. For many years, China banned foreigners from visiting Tibet, which its army occupied in 1950. Chinese rulers in Tibet made efforts to destroy traditional Tibetan culture and introduce Chinese ideas – a clear breach of Tibetan peoples' human rights. But, until outsiders knew what was happening, they were powerless to act.

Why don't we all demand our rights?

Sometimes, people facing problems do not think human rights could help them. A children's charity worker explained: 'In traditional societies … parents don't see the point of sending [children with disabilities] to school…' But by denying children their right to education, these parents are limiting their children's lives.

Starving families during the Somali famine of 1992. Tragically, the United Nations failed to save millions of people like these.

Do human rights workers make errors?

Sometimes, human rights organizations simply make the wrong decisions, or fail to achieve what they set out to do. For example, the United Nations sent troops to Somalia in 1992, to stop the civil war that had led to a human rights crisis with six million people starving. The United Nations tried, but failed, to protect aid workers and to make peace between rival warlords. In 1995, after many UN soldiers were killed, United Nations troops were forced to retreat, having failed in their mission.

DEBATE - If we know about human rights abuses, do we have a duty to put them right?

- Yes. We should do all we can to help abused people, by joining campaigning organizations, writing letters or voting for politicians who support human rights.
- No. Our chief responsibility is to our family, our local community and our nation. We can't take on the problems of people all round the world.

Inspecting oil pipelines in the Arabia desert. Saudi Arabia is the world's largest supplier of oil. Its wealth gives it the power to choose whether or not to abide by human rights laws.

Why don't people do more?

Supporters of human rights are often not free to act exactly as they would like. Individual human rights campaigners do not have much power when faced with hostile governments, and they are often short of money to finance their protests. Many humanitarian organizations deliberately do not protest about lack of human rights, for fear of offending governments in countries where they work. They concentrate on practical projects, such as healthcare or feeding schemes, and this work saves millions of lives.

Why do governments ignore rights?

Often, governments let commercial or political interests affect their view of civil rights issues. They will turn a blind eye to human rights abuses in countries that are political allies, or trading partners. For example, in 1998, Human Rights Watch reported that 'Saudi Arabia and its oil-rich strategically

useful neighbours faced no public pressure [from the US government] on their own records of repression... Israeli [human rights] abuses, if mentioned at all, were treated as 'obstacles to peace' rather than human rights violations...'

Some governments even break their own laws, to make money or avoid social problems. For example, in 1996, Mexican women working in factories in Export Processing Zones were subjected to regular humiliating physical tests, and dismissed if they were found to be pregnant. This clearly broke Mexico's labour laws, which banned sex discrimination, but government officials refused to enforce them. The Zones provided jobs for over half a million workers, who would otherwise be unemployed, and earned almost US$30 billion in exports – a great boost to the Mexican economy.

Could the UN do more?

The United Nations is sometimes accused of acting too slowly and too late. UN bureaucracy can take years to reach decisions, and sometimes gives in to pressure from powerful nations. For example, an official UN enquiry into the horrific genocide in Rwanda in 1994, when militias made up of the majority Hutu tribe killed over 800 000 members of the minority Tutsi tribe, found that the UN Secretary General 'made weak and equivocal [uncertain] decisions in the face of mounting disaster'. Also, the Security Council had withdrawn UN peace-keeping troops when it should have sent more, probably because of pressure from the USA and Belgium. It concluded that UN inaction had worsened the situation, and led to many Tutsi deaths.

Canadian troops with Rwandan refugee children, June 1994. The soldiers were part of a UN force trying to restore peace, law and order after the terrible massacres earlier in the year. Although these troops are doing their best to help, the UN was strongly criticized for failing to take action to prevent the massacres happening.

DEBATE – Should governments support human rights even if it damages their economic interests?

- Yes. Human rights are more important than money.
- No. A government must do all it can to make its country prosperous.

Who Has The Duty To Defend Human Rights?

People suffering from human rights abuses are often unable to help themselves – they may be prisoners, or slaves, or homeless refugees. Who should work with them to gain their rights?

Jose Ramos Horta (left) and Bishop Bello (right) campaigned for human rights in East Timor. Their work won them the Nobel Peace Prize in 1996.

THE UNIVERSAL DECLARATION of Human Rights states that all 'individuals, groups, and organs of society' have a duty to encourage human rights. In practice, human rights action is often left to a few brave individuals, such as Rigoberta Menchu (see pages 4–5), or to dedicated campaigning groups, such as Amnesty International and Human Rights Watch. A bewildering number of official organizations also have human rights responsibilities. These include government departments, such as Ministries for Women now found in many countries; independent monitors, such as the UK's Disability Rights Commission; international organizations, such as the International Labour Organization; and bodies administering international agreements, such as the European Social Charter (drawn up in 1961 to protect human rights in member states of the Council of Europe). Plus, of course, the United Nations itself! Getting them all to agree on action, or to work together, can be an impossible task.

What role does money play?

International financial organizations also claim a share of the responsibility. The World Bank, which was set up by the UN in 1945, lends money and encourages businesses in developing countries. Although it has often been criticized for its economic policies and for burdening poor countries with expensive debts, it has declared its commitment to working for human rights.

According to many human rights campaigners, multinational companies also have a responsibility to contribute to the growth and protection of human rights. In 1999, UN Secretary General Kofi Annan encouraged business leaders to sign up to the 'Global Compact', an international agreement linking human rights to the growth of global trade. The Body Shop is a well-known example of a multinational company taking an active role in promoting human rights and community trade – believing that big businesses have an important role to play in bringing about social and environmental change. Often in partnership with Amnesty International, the Body Shop actively campaigns for people whose human rights are denied, and it has set up a Human Rights Award to help work on issues such as child labour and housing.

'As you move through your day at work or school or home, pause to ask yourself if all your rights and freedoms are fully respected. Are the rights of those around you respected? If not, why? Can you change something by letting someone know that the standards set forth in the Universal Declaration of Human Rights are not being met?'

Source: National Co-ordinating Committee for UNDHR 50/Franklin and Eleanor Roosevelt Institute, 1998

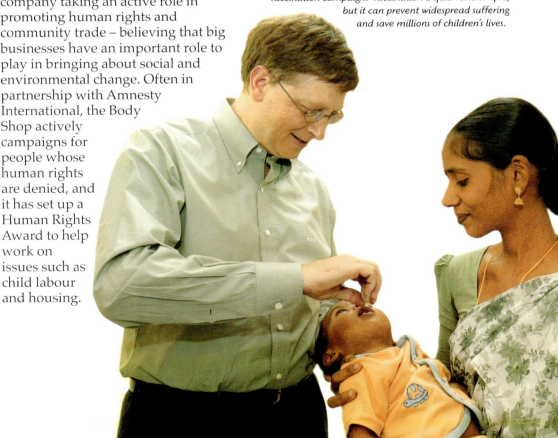

Bill Gates (left), founder of Microsoft, one of the richest companies in the world, has set up a foundation to help bring the human right of healthcare to people in developing countries. He is shown here giving a dose of polio vaccine to a young child in India, as part of a mass vaccination campaign. Vaccination is quick and simple, but it can prevent widespread suffering and save millions of children's lives.

Who else can help?

The media plays an important part in safeguarding and promoting human rights. It does this in several ways. Journalists have the skills to investigate human rights abuses that have been deliberately concealed. They can give publicity to human rights campaigners, and help them win more supporters. They can subject human rights abusers to hostile questioning, and expose them to criticism and contempt from people all round the world. However, this work is not without danger, and many journalists and other media workers, such as photographers, are killed or threatened each year.

Can famous people help?

Famous public figures can also help human rights, by bringing publicity and encouraging support. For example, UNICEF (the United Nations Children's Fund) regularly appoints well-known people, such as singer Robbie Williams and actress Susan Sarandon, to be special ambassadors. UNICEF sends them to visit areas where it is working for children's rights. In India, famous Booker prize-winning novelist Arundhati Roy has risked prison sentences by taking part in campaigns to protect the rights of poor local people whose heritage, homes and livelihood were threatened by massive dam-building schemes.

Casualties of reporting the truth

* In 2002, forty-six journalists and other media workers were killed worldwide because of their work.
* Colombia is the most dangerous country in the world in which to be a journalist – 10 were murdered there in 2002.
* Russia was the second most dangerous country, with seven violent deaths in 2002.

Source: Canadian Journalists for Free Expression (CJFE), annual report 2002

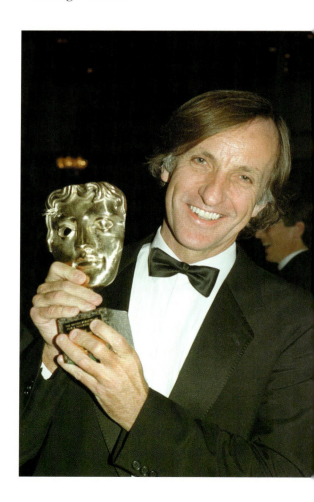

Campaigning journalist John Pilger is well-known for his work in raising awareness of human rights abuses in many parts of the world. He received the BAFTA Award for Investigative Journalism in 1991.

Does religion affect human rights?

Religious leaders have sometimes been responsible for human rights abuses. For example, the Muslim Taliban government in Afghanistan denied basic freedoms to many citizens. But other religious leaders, like the Buddhist Dalai Lama, have seen it as their duty to use their powerful influence to campaign for human rights, especially religious freedom and respect for indigenous cultures.

In the late twentieth century, Christian churches played a leading part in the Jubilee 2000 movement, which called for rich countries to cancel debts owed to them by developing nations. Here, supporters of Jubilee 2000, carrying huge crosses, protest outside a meeting of the World Bank.

Pope calls for abolition of death penalty

Roman Catholic Pope John Paul II, who often holds conservative opinions on social matters, used human rights language when he called for the abolition of the death penalty in 1999:
'Modern society has the means of protecting itself, without denying criminals the chance to reform. The death penalty is cruel and unnecessary ... even in the case of someone who has done great evil.'

Source: New York Times, *28 January 1999*

How Can Human Rights Abusers Be Punished?

In peaceful countries, where there are fair and honest laws, people who feel deprived of their human rights can take employers, organizations, or even governments to court. But in wartime, or in countries with repressive governments, this is not possible. It can also be very difficult for people in one country to take action against human rights abusers in another land.

Growing numbers of shoppers choose "Fairtrade" products because they know that companies producing them respect workers' rights.

HOWEVER, THERE ARE ways of taking action. In the 1970s and 1980s, many nations, companies, and individual consumers took part in a boycott of South African goods to protest against the apartheid system. They refused to buy South African goods or sell aircraft and weapons to South African armed forces.

Trade arrangements have also been used to put pressure on governments with poor human rights records. Since the 1970s, the US has refused to grant "Most Favored Nation" status, which gives major business advantages, to many countries with repressive governments. These include Afghanistan, Albania, Cambodia, Cuba, and North Korea. Many American politicians and human rights campaigners also called for China to be included on the list, but American presidents argued that the mere threat of being excluded from trade with the US was enough to force China to improve human rights.

In 2001, Serbian leader Slobodan Milosevic was accused of violating many human rights, and sent for trial at the International War Crimes Tribunal in The Hague, Netherlands.

Can laws cross boundaries?

There are legal methods of punishing human rights abusers, even at a distance. For example, the European Court of Justice has the power to try all alleged breaches of European Union law, including human rights crimes. Citizens of many EU member nations have challenged their own governments' actions in the court, and many have won. This court works because EU member states recognize its authority.

To punish human rights abusers in war-torn countries, such as Rwanda and former Yugoslavia, the United Nations has set up Tribunals (temporary special courts) to try army leaders and soldiers accused of war crimes. These Tribunals work because they are backed up by the threat of military action, and economic sanctions as well.

Since 1945, there has been an International Court of Justice, in The Hague in the Netherlands. It is part of the United Nations, with judges from many nations elected by the Security Council and the General Assembly. But it is mainly concerned with settling disputes between UN member nations. So, in 1998, the United Nations resolved to set up a special new court, the International Criminal Court, with the power to try human rights abusers from all member nations who agree to accept the court's powers.

Rich countries put pressure on the poor

"The United States is warning Eritrea and Swaziland that they will lose preferential trade and investment privileges unless they improve human rights and other conditions in their countries... Swaziland is facing multiple crises ... and the monarch's purchase of a $45 million executive jet is criticized by aid agencies as an extravagance when 25 percent of the population is facing food shortages."

Source: Sapa-AFP

DEBATE—Do you think it is right that some countries, like the US, refuse to recognize the International Criminal Court?

- Yes. They want their own laws to be supreme.
- No. We need special international courts to enforce human rights laws in countries where they are not part of national law-codes.

Can human rights abusers change?

By itself, the Universal Declaration of Human Rights has no power. But, during the late twentieth century, many people who supported human rights ideas found other ways of making human rights abusers change their behaviour.

Can political persuasion work?

One of the most powerful 'weapons' in the fight for human rights is collective action by groups of nations. They can force all their members to accept human rights as a condition of joining their group. For example, Turkey's application to join the European Union was turned down in 2002 because leaders of the EU felt that Turkish people still did not have full human rights. Actions like this can persuade governments that are not keen supporters of human rights to improve their citizens' lives. They see agreeing to human rights as a fair price to pay for the political and economic benefits that belonging to the larger group will bring.

Does international aid make a difference?

International aid can also be used to fight for human rights. For example, in the late 1990s in East Timor, the Indonesian army and police took no action when armed gangs attacked civilians who had voted for independence. The killings prompted a forceful letter, threatening to withdraw aid, from the President of the World Bank, which had loaned the Indonesian government vast sums of money. The President wrote: 'For the international financial community to be able to continue its full support, it is critical that you act swiftly to restore order and that your government carry out its public commitment to honour the referendum outcome.'

A Kurdish woman, whose family has been killed by Turkish special forces, pleads with them not to shoot. The Turkish government has been accused of many human rights abuses, especially against the Kurdish minority population, since this photo was taken in 1993.

The impressive headquarters of the wealthy European Union in Brussels, Belgium. Countries wishing to join the European Union have to agree to support human rights ideals, and to introduce human rights policies into their laws.

Does self-interest have a role?

Finally, human rights abusers can often be made to reform once they realize that it is in their own interest to do so. This was summed up very well by US Secretary of State Cyrus Vance, speaking in 1977. 'We seek these [human rights] goals because they are right – and because we, too, will benefit. Our own well-being, and even our security, are enhanced [made better] in a world that shares common freedoms and in which prosperity and economic justice create the conditions for peace.'

Human rights organizations vow to continue their work

'You can intimidate the prisoner; you can frighten the immigrant; you can silence the refugee, but we will not be intimidated and we will not be frightened and we will not be silenced. We will stand up for freedom and security and human rights. And we will prevail.'

Source: Stand Up for Freedom, Security and Human Rights, by William F. Schulz, Executive Director of Amnesty International USA

DEBATE - 'If you're not part of the solution, you must be part of the problem.' Do you agree that we all have a duty to protect and encourage human rights?

- Yes. Enforcing human rights ideals will make the world a better place for everyone.
- No. Human rights activists are busy-bodies. Human rights ideals get in the way of an individual country's laws, encourage refugees and slow down international trade.

REFERENCE

THE UNIVERSAL DECLARATION OF HUMAN RIGHTS, 1948

Whereas recognition of the inherent dignity and of the equal and inalienable rights of all members of the human family is the foundation of freedom, justice and peace in the world,

Whereas disregard and contempt for human rights have resulted in barbarous acts which have outraged the conscience of mankind, and the advent of a world in which human beings shall enjoy freedom of speech and belief and freedom from fear and want has been proclaimed as the highest aspiration of the common people,

Whereas it is essential, if man is not to be compelled to have recourse, as a last resort, to rebellion against tyranny and oppression, that human rights should be protected by the rule of law,

Whereas it is essential to promote the development of friendly relations between nations,

Whereas the peoples of the United Nations have in the Charter reaffirmed their faith in fundamental human rights, in the dignity and worth of the human person and in the equal rights of men and women and have determined to promote social progress and better standards of life in larger freedom,

Whereas Member States have pledged themselves to achieve, in cooperation with the United Nations, the promotion of universal respect for and observance of human rights and fundamental freedoms,

Whereas a common understanding of these rights and freedoms is of the greatest importance for the full realization of this pledge,

Now, therefore, The General Assembly, Proclaims this Universal Declaration of Human Rights as a common standard of achievement for all peoples and all nations, to the end that every individual and every organ of society, keeping this Declaration constantly in mind, shall strive by teaching and education to promote respect for these rights and freedoms and by progressive measures, national and international, to secure their universal and effective recognition and observance, both among the peoples of Member States themselves and among the peoples of territories under their jurisdiction.

ARTICLE 1

All human beings are born free and equal in dignity and rights. They are endowed with reason and conscience and should act towards one another in a spirit of brotherhood.

ARTICLE 2

Everyone is entitled to all the rights and freedoms set forth in this Declaration, without distinction of any kind, such as race, colour, sex, language, religion, political or other opinion, national or social origin, property, birth or other status. Furthermore, no distinction shall be made on the basis of the political, jurisdictional or international status of the country or territory to which a person belongs, whether it be independent, trust, non-self-governing or under any other limitation of sovereignty.

ARTICLE 3

Everyone has the right to life, liberty and security of person.

ARTICLE 4

No one shall be held in slavery or

servitude; slavery and the slave trade shall be prohibited in all their forms.

ARTICLE 5
No one shall be subjected to torture or to cruel, inhuman or degrading treatment or punishment.

ARTICLE 6
Everyone has the right to recognition everywhere as a person before the law.

ARTICLE 7
All are equal before the law and are entitled without any discrimination to equal protection of the law. All are entitled to equal protection against any discrimination in violation of this Declaration and against any incitement to such discrimination.

ARTICLE 8
Everyone has the right to an effective remedy by the competent national tribunals for acts violating the fundamental rights granted him by the constitution or by law.

ARTICLE 9
No one shall be subjected to arbitrary arrest, detention or exile.

ARTICLE 10
Everyone is entitled in full equality to a fair and public hearing by an independent and impartial tribunal, in the determination of his rights and obligations and of any criminal charge against him.

ARTICLE 11
1. Everyone charged with a penal offence has the right to be presumed innocent until proved guilty according to law in a public trial at which he has had all the guarantees necessary for his defence.
2. No one shall be held guilty of any penal offence on account of any act or omission which did not constitute a penal offence, under national or international law, at the time when it was committed. Nor shall a heavier penalty be imposed than the one that was applicable at the time the penal offence was committed.

ARTICLE 12
No one shall be subjected to arbitrary interference with his privacy, family, home or correspondence, nor to attacks upon his honour and reputation. Everyone has the right to the protection of the law against such interference or attacks.

ARTICLE 13
1. Everyone has the right to freedom of movement and residence within the borders of each State.
2. Everyone has the right to leave any country, including his own, and to return to his country.

ARTICLE 14
1. Everyone has the right to seek and to enjoy in other countries asylum from persecution.
2. This right may not be invoked in the case of prosecutions genuinely arising from non-political crimes or from acts contrary to the purposes and principles of the United Nations.

ARTICLE 15
1. Everyone has the right to a nationality.
2. No one shall be arbitrarily deprived of his nationality nor denied the right to change his nationality.

ARTICLE 16

1. Men and women of full age, without any limitation due to race, nationality or religion, have the right to marry and to found a family. They are entitled to equal rights as to marriage, during marriage and at its dissolution.
2. Marriage shall be entered into only with the free and full consent of the intending spouses.
3. The family is the natural and fundamental group unit of society and is entitled to protection by society and the State.

ARTICLE 17

1. Everyone has the right to own property alone as well as in association with others.
2. No one shall be arbitrarily deprived of his property.

ARTICLE 18

Everyone has the right to freedom of thought, conscience and religion; this right includes freedom to change his religion or belief, and freedom, either alone or in community with others and in public or private, to manifest his religion or belief in teaching, practice, worship and observance.

ARTICLE 19

Everyone has the right to freedom of opinion and expression; this right includes freedom to hold opinions without interference and to seek, receive and impart information and ideas through any media and regardless of frontiers.

ARTICLE 20

1. Everyone has the right to freedom of peaceful assembly and association.
2. No one may be compelled to belong to an association.

ARTICLE 21

1. Everyone has the right to take part in the government of his country, directly or through freely chosen representatives.
2. Everyone has the right to equal access to public service in his country.
3. The will of the people shall be the basis of the authority of government; this will shall be expressed in periodic and genuine elections which shall be by universal and equal suffrage and shall be held by secret vote or by equivalent free voting procedures.

ARTICLE 22

Everyone, as a member of society, has the right to social security and is entitled to realization, through national effort and international co-operation and in accordance with the organization and resources of each State, of the economic, social and cultural rights indispensable for his dignity and the free development of his personality.

ARTICLE 23

1. Everyone has the right to work, to free choice of employment, to just and favourable conditions of work and to protection against unemployment.
2. Everyone, without any discrimination, has the right to equal pay for equal work.
3. Everyone who works has the right to just and favourable remuneration ensuring for himself and his family an existence worthy of human dignity, and supplemented, if necessary, by other means of social protection.
4. Everyone has the right to form and to join trade unions for the protection of his interests.

ARTICLE 24

Everyone has the right to rest and leisure, including reasonable limitation of working hours and periodic holidays with pay.

ARTICLE 25

1. Everyone has the right to a standard of living adequate for the health and well-being of himself and of his family, including food, clothing, housing and medical care and necessary social services, and the right to security in the event of unemployment, sickness, disability, widowhood, old age or other lack of livelihood in circumstances beyond his control.

2. Motherhood and childhood are entitled to special care and assistance. All children, whether born in or out of wedlock, shall enjoy the same social protection.

ARTICLE 26

1. Everyone has the right to education. Education shall be free, at least in the elementary and fundamental stages. Elementary education shall be compulsory. Technical and professional education shall be made generally available and higher education shall be equally accessible to all on the basis of merit.

2. Education shall be directed to the full development of the human personality and to the strengthening of respect for human rights and fundamental freedoms. It shall promote understanding, tolerance and friendship among all nations, racial or religious groups, and shall further the activities of the United Nations for the maintenance of peace.

3. Parents have a prior right to choose the kind of education that shall be given to their children.

ARTICLE 27

1. Everyone has the right freely to participate in the cultural life of the community, to enjoy the arts and to share in scientific advancement and its benefits.

2. Everyone has the right to the protection of the moral and material interests resulting from any scientific, literary or artistic production of which he is the author.

ARTICLE 28

Everyone is entitled to a social and international order in which the rights and freedoms set forth in this Declaration can be fully realized.

ARTICLE 29

1. Everyone has duties to the community in which alone the free and full development of his personality is possible.

2. In the exercise of his rights and freedoms, everyone shall be subject only to such limitations as are determined by law solely for the purpose of securing due recognition and respect for the rights and freedoms of others and of meeting the just requirements of morality, public order and the general welfare in a democratic society.

3. These rights and freedoms may in no case be exercised contrary to the purposes and principles of the United Nations.

ARTICLE 30

Nothing in this Declaration may be interpreted as implying for any State, group or person any right to engage in any activity or to perform any act aimed at the destruction of any of the rights and freedoms set forth herein.

GLOSSARY

activist Someone who campaigns or works for a certain cause, such as human rights.

adultery To have sex with someone other than your husband or wife.

apartheid Literally meaning 'apartness', the political policies of the South African government from 1948 until the early 1990s designed to keep peoples segregated based on their colour.

asylum A place of safety and refuge usually provided by a country for those seeking refugee status.

colony A country or region ruled by another country.

communism A system, or the belief in a system, in which capitalism is overthrown and control of wealth and property belongs to the state.

co-operation To work together.

covenant A legally binding agreement, or treaty.

culture The traditions, values, lifestyles and beliefs shared by a group of people.

democracy A country in which the people can vote to choose those who govern them.

detention centre A place where people claiming asylum and refugee status are held whilst their case is investigated.

dictatorship A country ruled by a person with absolute power.

discrimination The act of treating people worse because they belong to a particular group.

ethnic cleansing An attempt to rid a country, or region, of a particular ethnic group. The term was first used to describe the attempt by Serb nationalists to rid Bosnia of Muslims.

ethnic group A group of people who share the same distinct culture, religion, way of life or language.

forced labour To make someone work, usually against their will, and under harsh conditions.

guerrilla A member of an unofficial military force, usually with some political aim such as the overthrow of a government.

house arrest To be detained in your own home, rather than in prison, under the constant watch of police or other government forces, such as the army.

human rights The rights that are regarded by most societies as belonging to everyone, such as the rights to freedom, justice and equality.

humanitarian Committed to improving the lives of other people.

immigrant Someone who moves to and settles in another country.

indigenous People who have lived in a country from earliest times, such as Australian Aborigines.

Islam The religion of Muslims, who follow the teachings of the seventh-century Prophet Muhammad.

micro-credit scheme A means of lending money at low interest rates to very poor people, who are not served by the big banks.

multinational Operating in many countries.

Nobel Peace Prize A prize given as the highest international recognition to a person, or persons, for work contributing to peace, or the improvement of human rights.

persecute To harass or ill-treat.

racism To discriminate against or attack a person, or a group of people, because of their skin colour.

reformist A person who wants to reform (make better) a country, or an institution, such as the police force, by ridding it of abuses or faults.

refugee Someone who is seeking safety, especially from war or persecution, by going to a foreign country.

repression The exertion of strict control over the freedom of others.

republic A country without a king or queen, such as the USA.

sanctions Measures taken against a country, such as the stopping of trade.

Soviet Union Also known as the USSR (Union of Soviet Socialist Republics), a country formed from the territories of the Russian Empire in 1917, which lasted until 1991.

tribunal A temporary court, usually set up to hear a specific case, such as an allegation of racial discrimination.

United Nations An international organization set up after the end of World War II to promote peace and co-operation throughout the world. Its predecessor was the League of Nations.

UN Security Council The permanent committee of the United Nations that oversees its peacekeeping operations around the world.

violation An abuse of something, such as a person's human rights.

World Bank An international financial organization, connected to the United Nations. It is the largest source of financial aid to developing countries.

World War I A war fought in Europe from 1914 to 1918, in which an alliance including Britain, France, Russia, Italy and the USA defeated the alliance of Germany, Austria-Hungary, Turkey and Bulgaria.

World War II A war fought in Europe, Africa and Asia from 1939 to 1945, in which an alliance including Britain, France, the Soviet Union and the USA defeated the alliance of Germany, Italy and Japan.

FURTHER INFORMATION

BOOKS

Rigoberta Menchu: Defending Human Rights by M. Silverstone and C. Bunch (Feminist Press, 1999)

Freedom! (Human Rights Information Pack) by Amnesty International (Hodder, 2001)

What's at Issue: Human Rights by Paul Wignell (Heinemann, 2001)

Freedom of Belief – What do we mean by Human Rights? by M. Hirst (Franklin Watts, 1997)

Stand Up for Your Rights! by Children from All Over the World (Two-Can Publishing, 2000)

World Organizations: Amnesty International by R. G. Grant (Franklin Watts, 2001)

Human Rights (Pacts and Treaties) by S. D. Gold (Twenty First Century Books, 1997)

Human Rights (Great Speeches in History) by L. Hitt (Greenhaven Press, 2001)

Human Rights: Opposing Viewpoints edited by M. E. Williams (Greenhaven Press, 1998)

Human Rights: Issues for a New Millennium by L. Jacobs Altman (Enslow Publishing, 2002)

ORGANIZATIONS

UK GOVERNMENT ORGANIZATIONS

The Commission for Racial Equality (CRE England)
Elliott House, 10/12 Allington Street
London SW1E 5EH
Website: www.cre.gov.uk

CRE Scotland
Hanover House, 45-51 Hanover Street
Edinburgh EH2 2PJ
Website: www.cre.gov.uk

CRE Wales
14 Floor, Capital Tower, Greyfriars Road
Cardiff CF1 3AG
Website: www.cre.gov.uk

The Equal Opportunities Commission (EOC England)
Arndale House, Arndale Centre
Manchester M4 3EQ
Website: www.eoc.org.uk

EOC Scotland
St Stephens House, 279 Bath Street
Glasgow G2 4JL
Website: www.eoc.org.uk

EOC Wales
Windsor House, Windsor Lane
Cardiff CF10 3GE
Website: www.eoc.org.uk

Disability Rights Commission
DRC Helpline, Freepost MID02164
Stratford-upon-Avon CV37 9BR
Website: www.drc-gb.org

Women's National Commission
Cabinet Office, 1st Floor
35 Great Smith Street
London SW1P 3BQ
Website: www.thewnc.org.uk

UK VOLUNTARY ORGANIZATIONS
For information on voluntary
organizations that work or campaign
for human rights, contact:

**National Council for Voluntary
Organizations (NCVO)**
Regent's Wharf, 8 All Saints Street
London N1 9RL
Website: www.ncvo-vol.org.uk

**Scottish Council for Voluntary
Organizations**
18/19 Claremont Crescent
Edinburgh EH7 4QD
Website: www.scvo.org.uk

INTERNATIONAL ORGANIZATIONS
Amnesty International
An organization that promotes general
awareness of human rights and opposes
specific abuses of human rights.
99-119 Rosebery Avenue
London EC1R 4RE, UK
Website: www.amnesty.org.uk

Human Rights Watch
A campaigning group that aims to
defend human rights worldwide.
350 Fifth Avenue, 34th Floor
New York, NY 10118-3299, USA
Website: www.hrw.org

United Nations Organization UK
3 Whitehall Court
London SW1A 2EL, UK
Website: www.una-uk.org

**United Nations Children's Fund
(UNICEF)**
Africa House, 64-67 Kingsway
London WC2B 6NB, UK
Website: www.unicef.org

Jubilee Research
A debt and finance programme that
supports economic justice campaigns
worldwide, especially cancellation of
debt in developing countries.
The New Economics Foundation,
Cinnamon House, 608 Cole Street
London SE1 4YH, UK
Website: www.jubileeplus.org

WEBSITES
www.unhcr.ch
Official site of the United Nations
High Commissioner for Refugees
The website has texts of all human
rights treaties and details of UN
proceedings (committee meetings,
press briefings, etc).

www.umn.edu/humanrts
University of Minnesota (USA) Human
Rights Library
A massive resource, with over 10 000
human rights documents and links to
over 3500 human rights websites.

www.oneworld.net
News and briefings on human rights
issues, plus links to over 1250
organizations working for human rights.

www.derechos.net
A human rights organization based in
Latin America, but with useful
information about human rights issues
in many parts of the world.

www.wdm.org.uk
Information about the World
Development Movement, a
campaigning group for human rights.

INDEX